I0513644

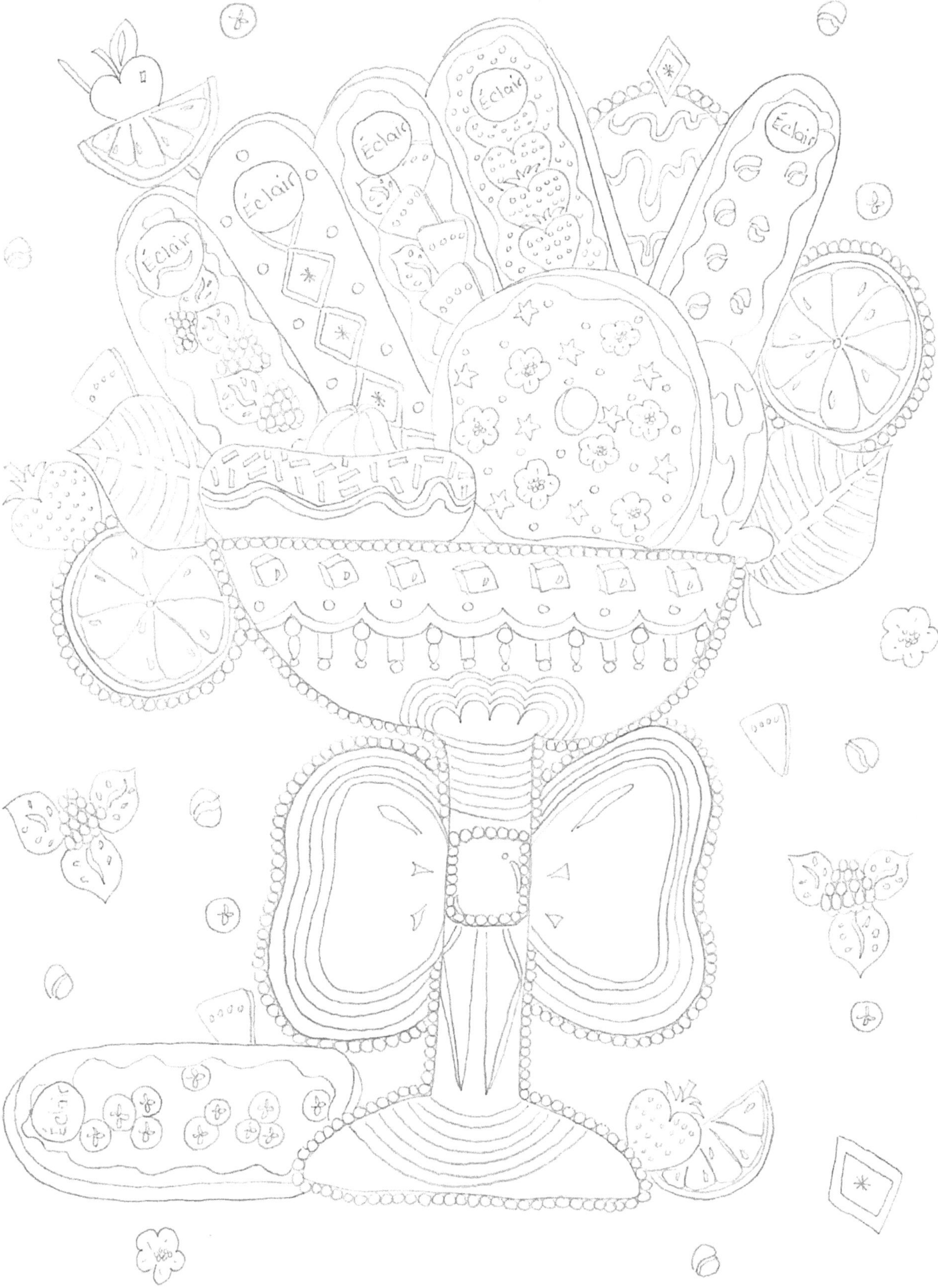

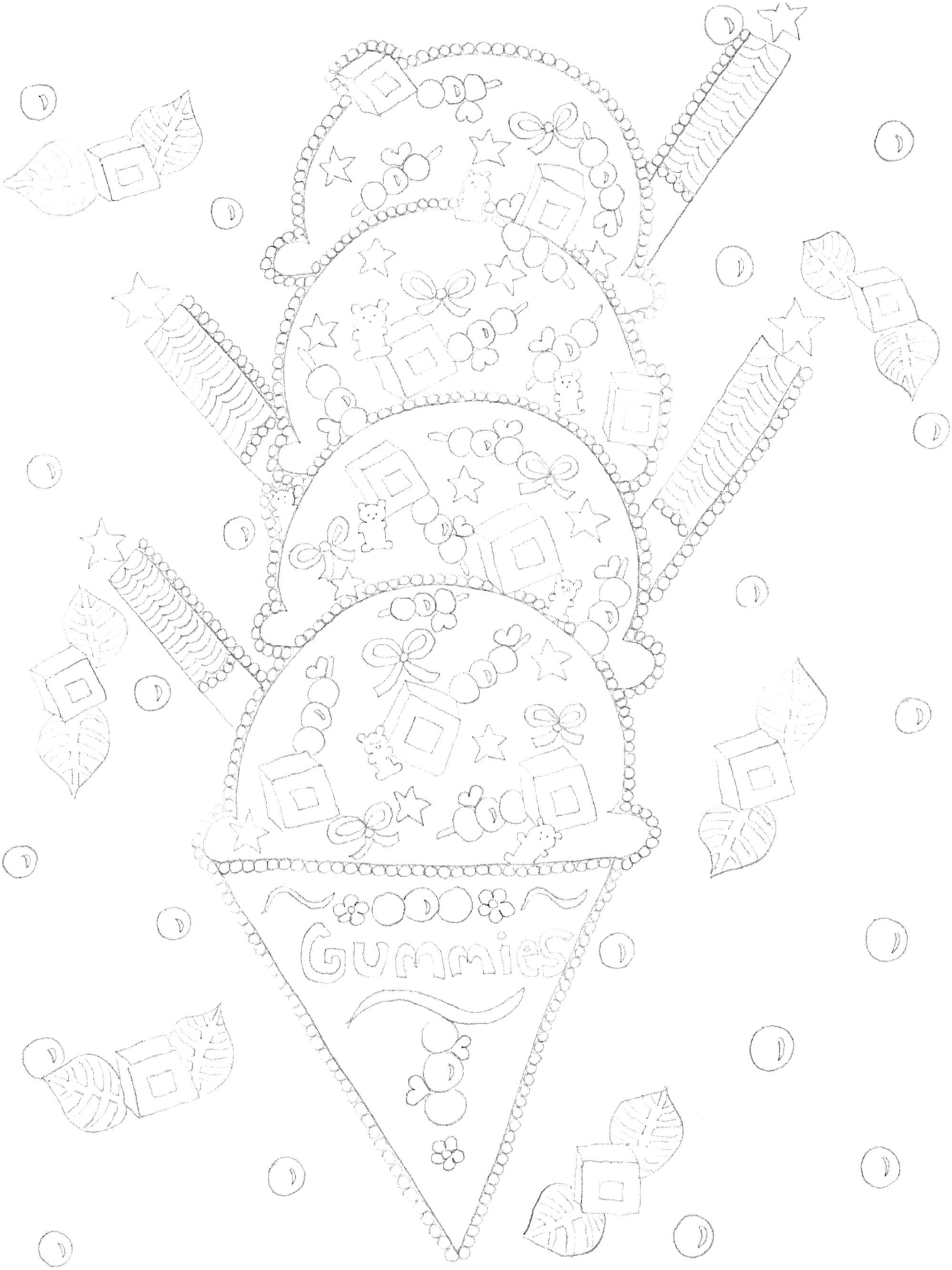
Gummies

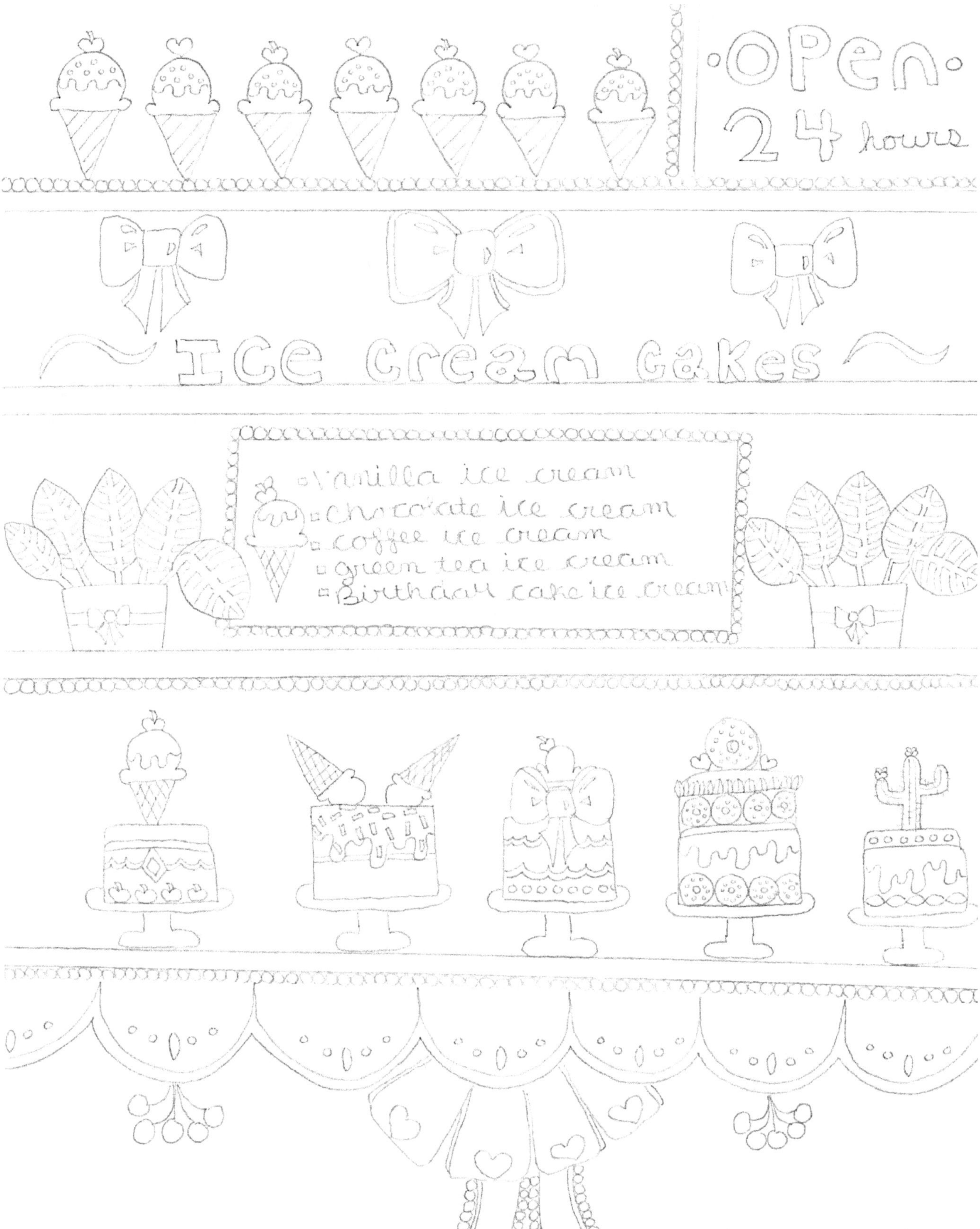
OPEN
24 hours
Ice Cream Cakes
Vanilla ice cream
Chocolate ice cream
coffee ice cream
green tea ice cream
Birthday cake ice cream

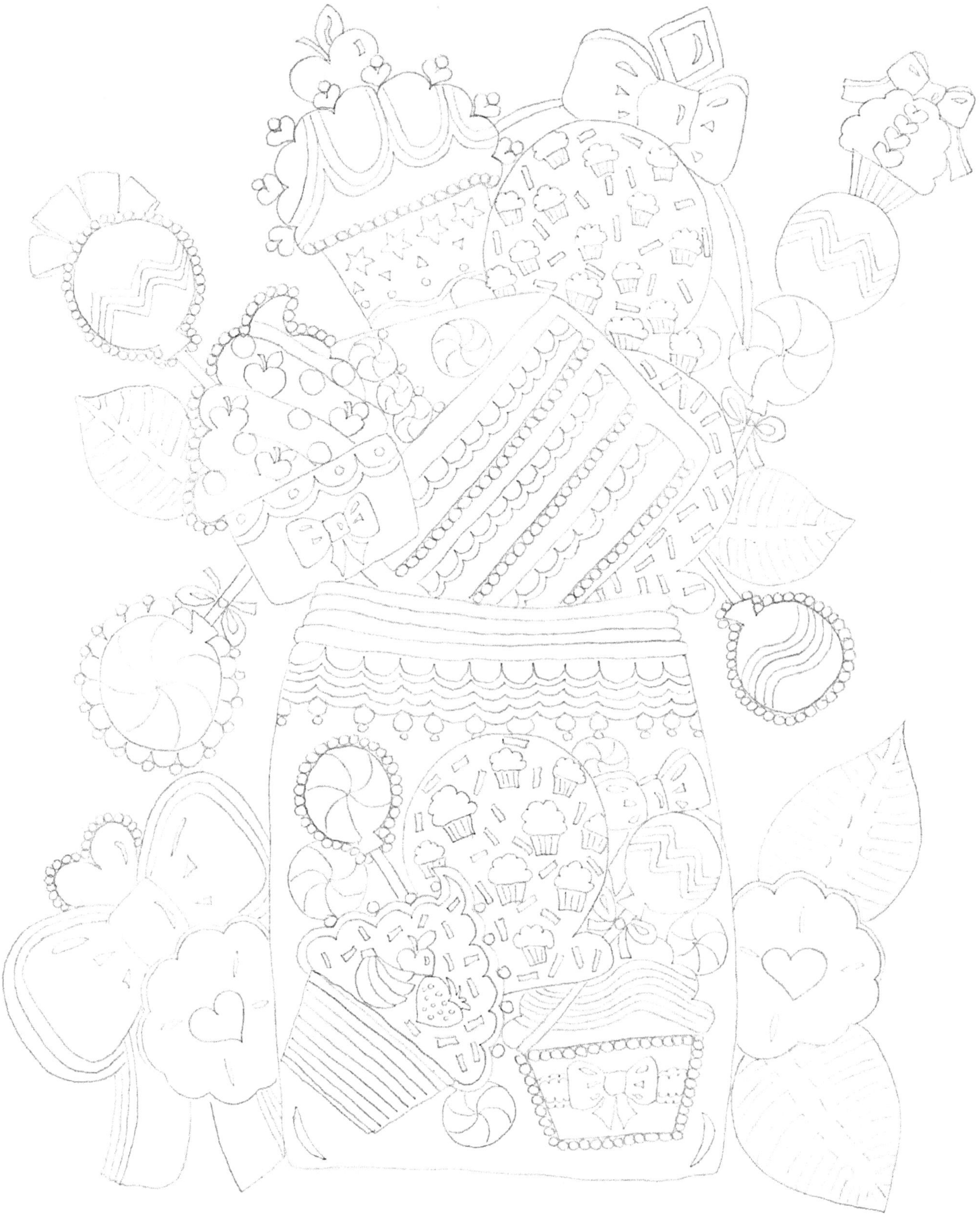

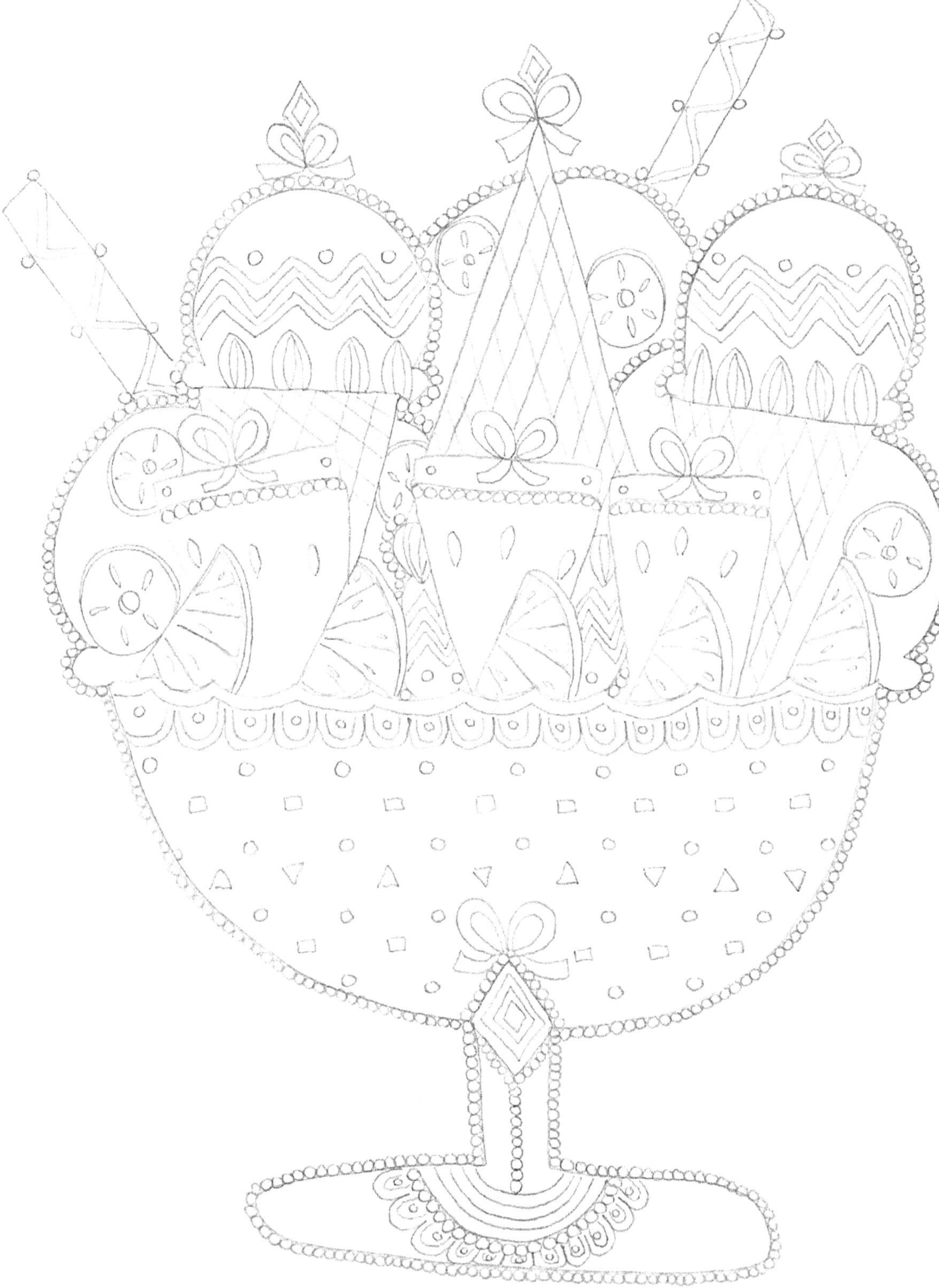

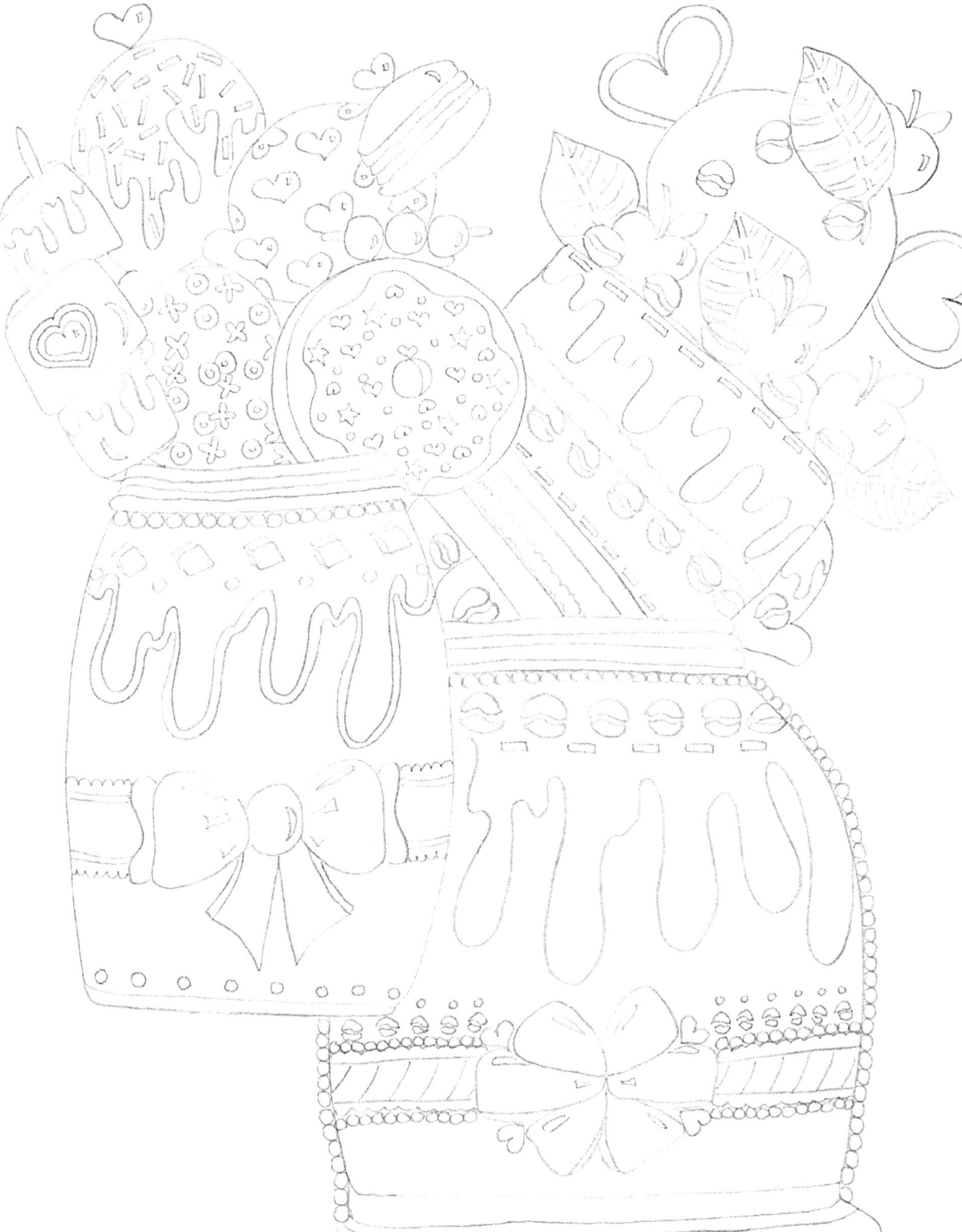

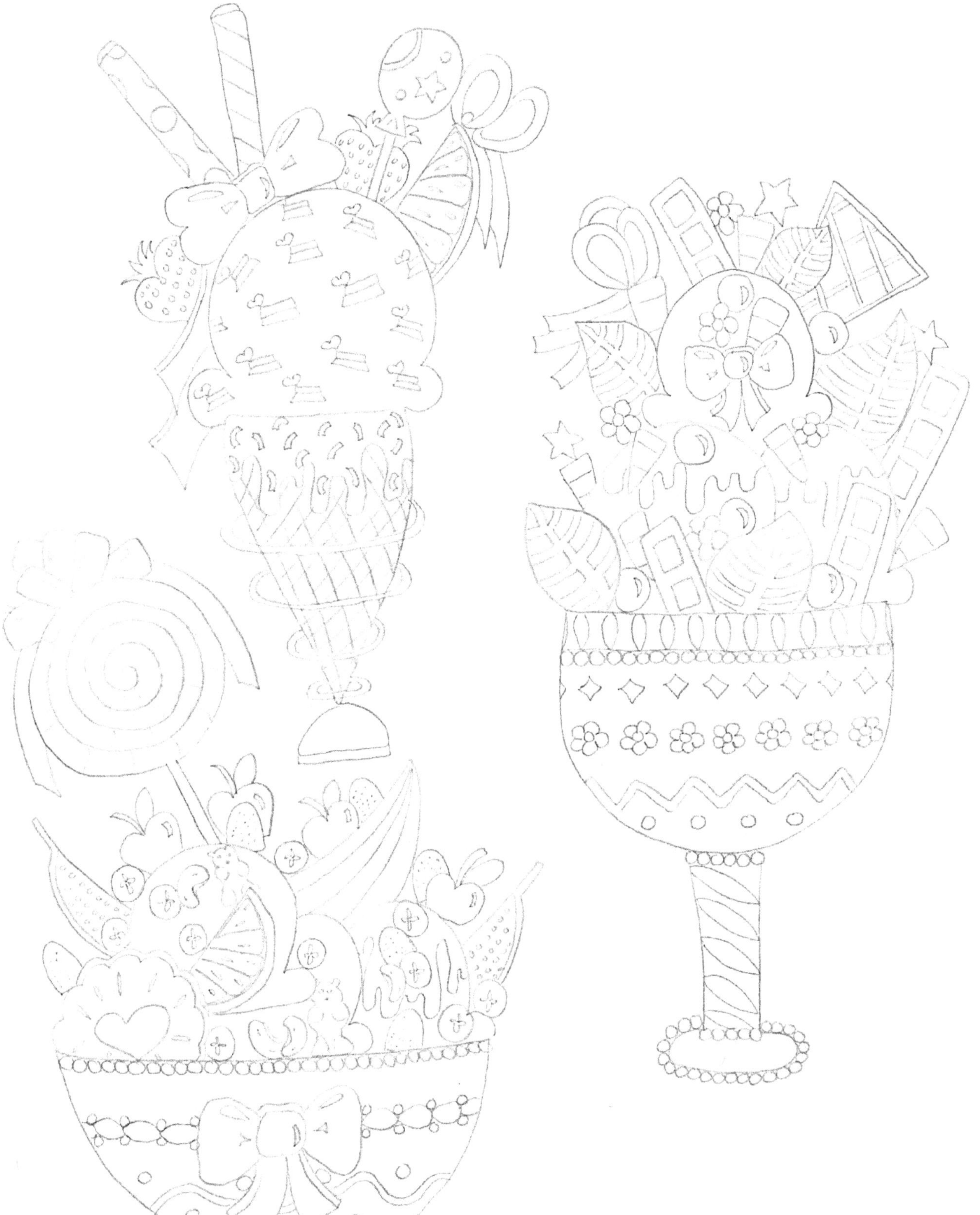

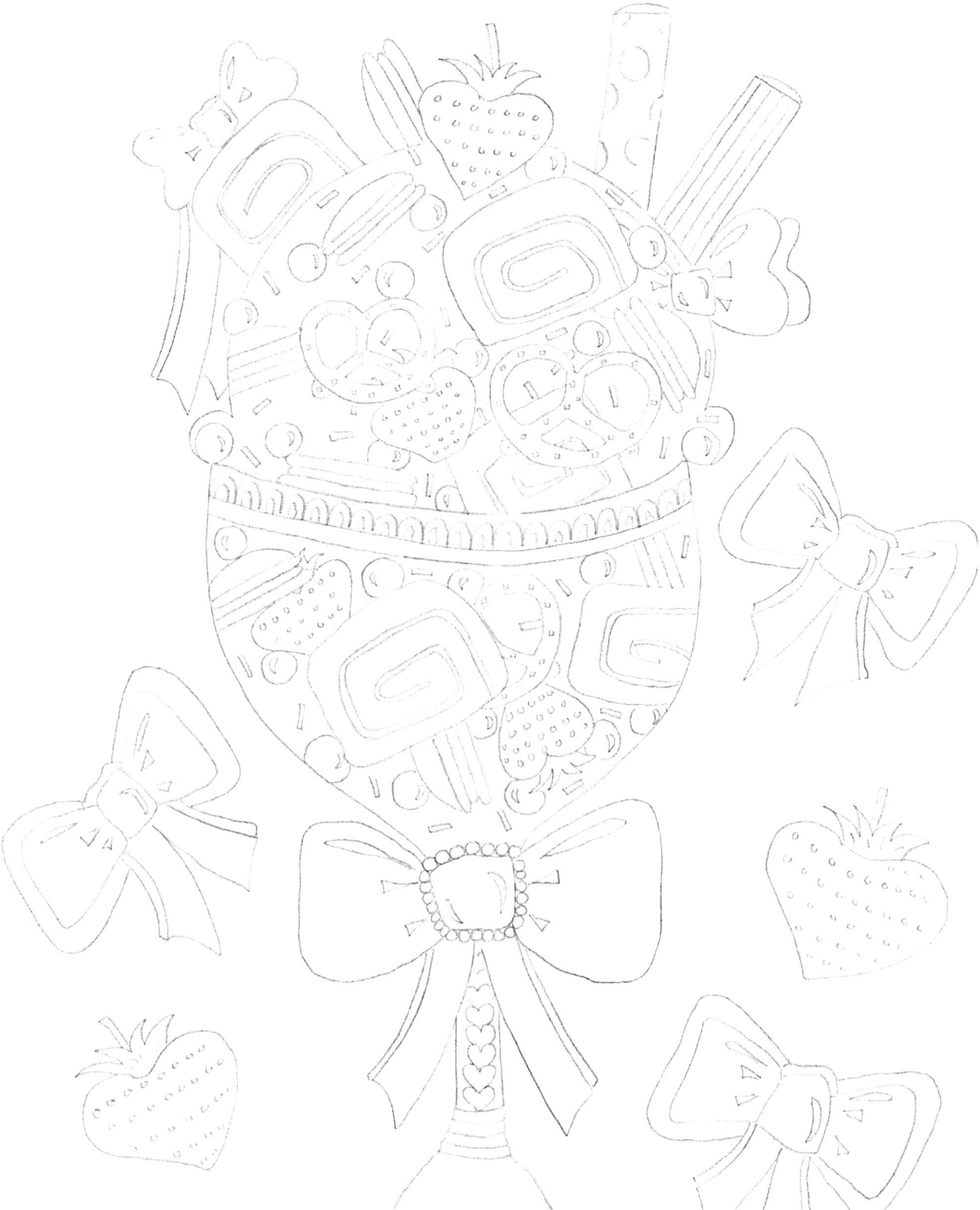

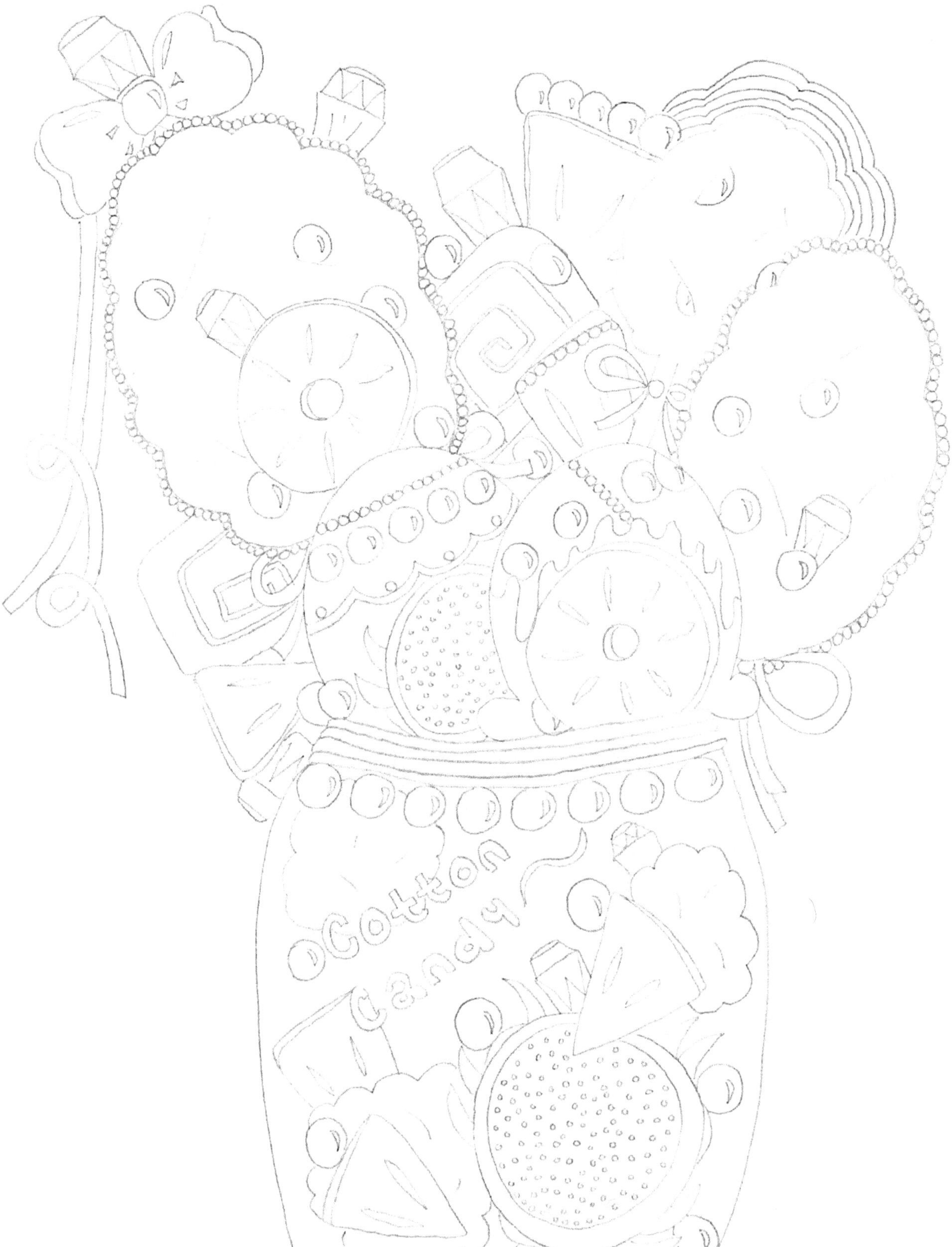
Cotton
Candy

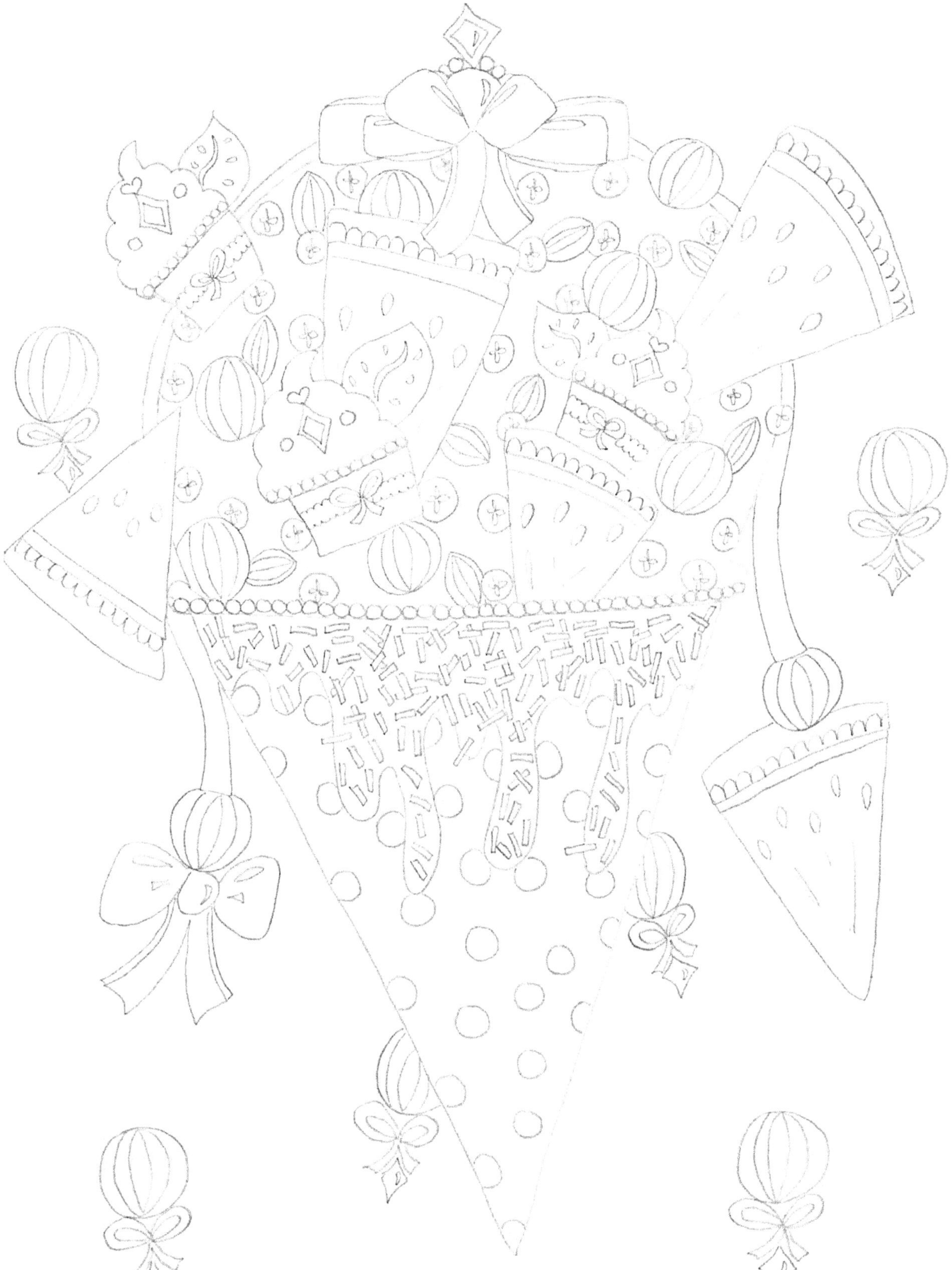

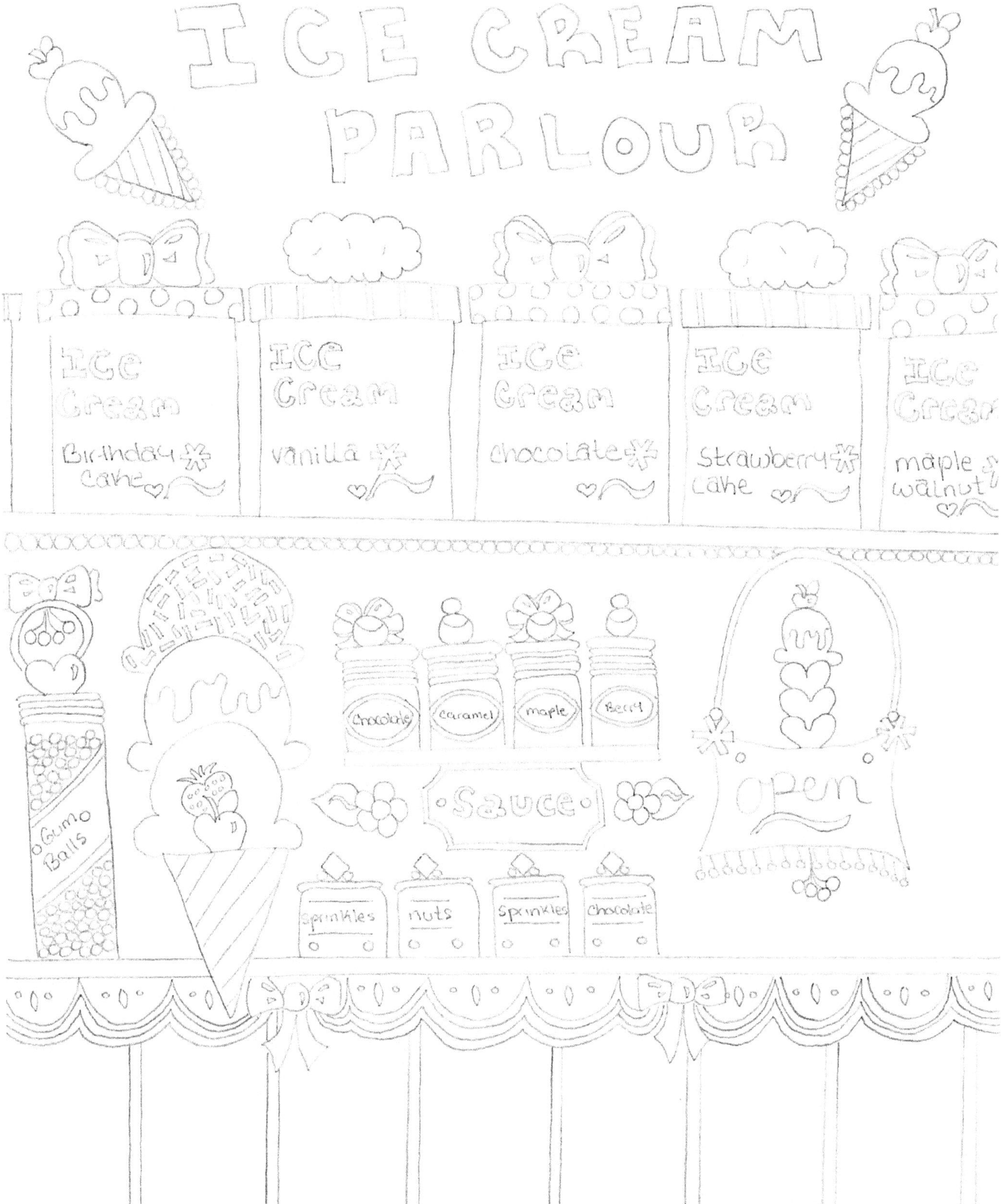
ICE CREAM
PARLOUR
Ice Cream
Birthday cake
Ice Cream
vanilla
Ice Cream
chocolate
Ice Cream
strawberry cake
Ice Cream
maple walnut
Gum Balls
chocolate
caramel
maple
Berry
Sauce
open
sprinkles
nuts
sprinkles
chocolate

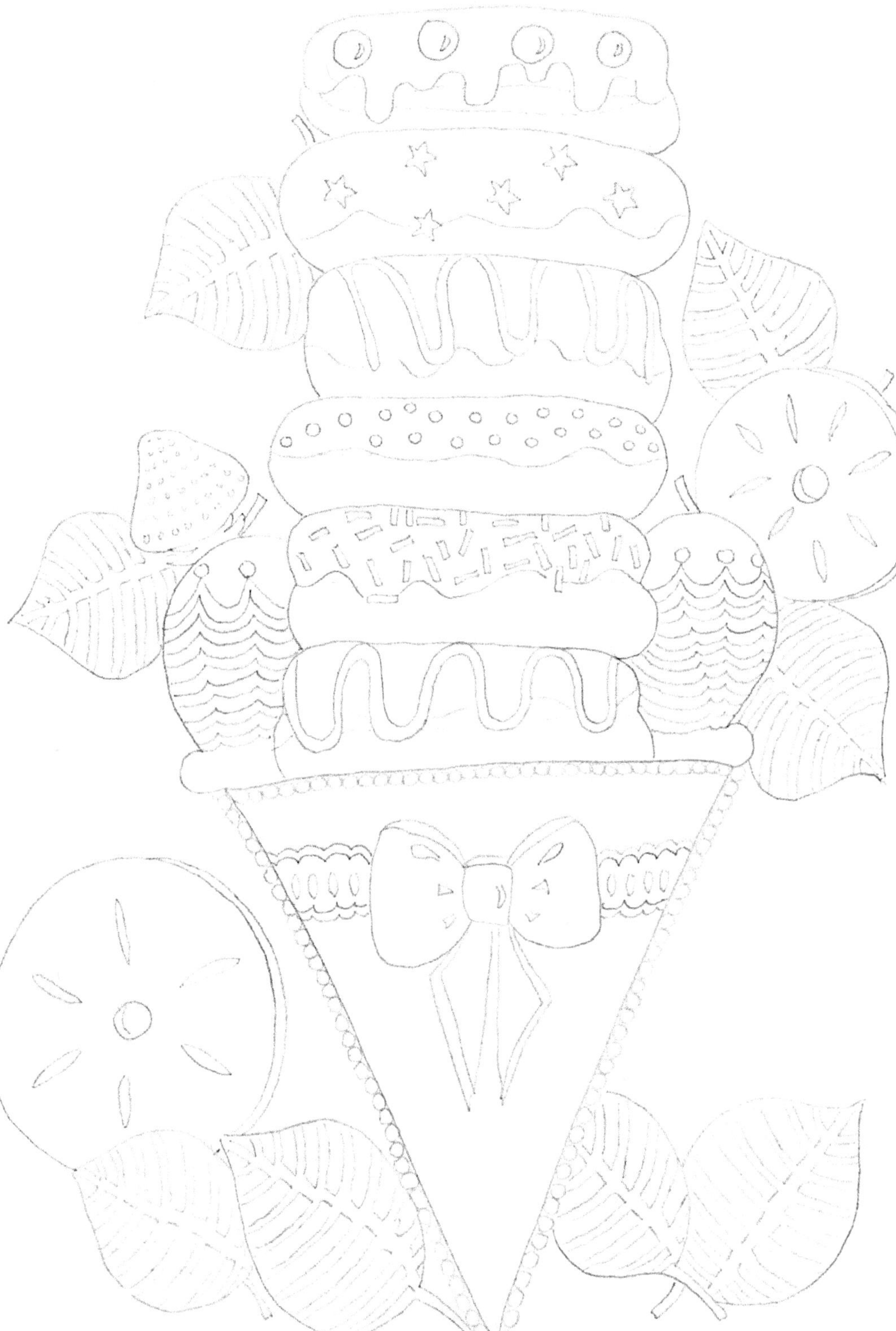

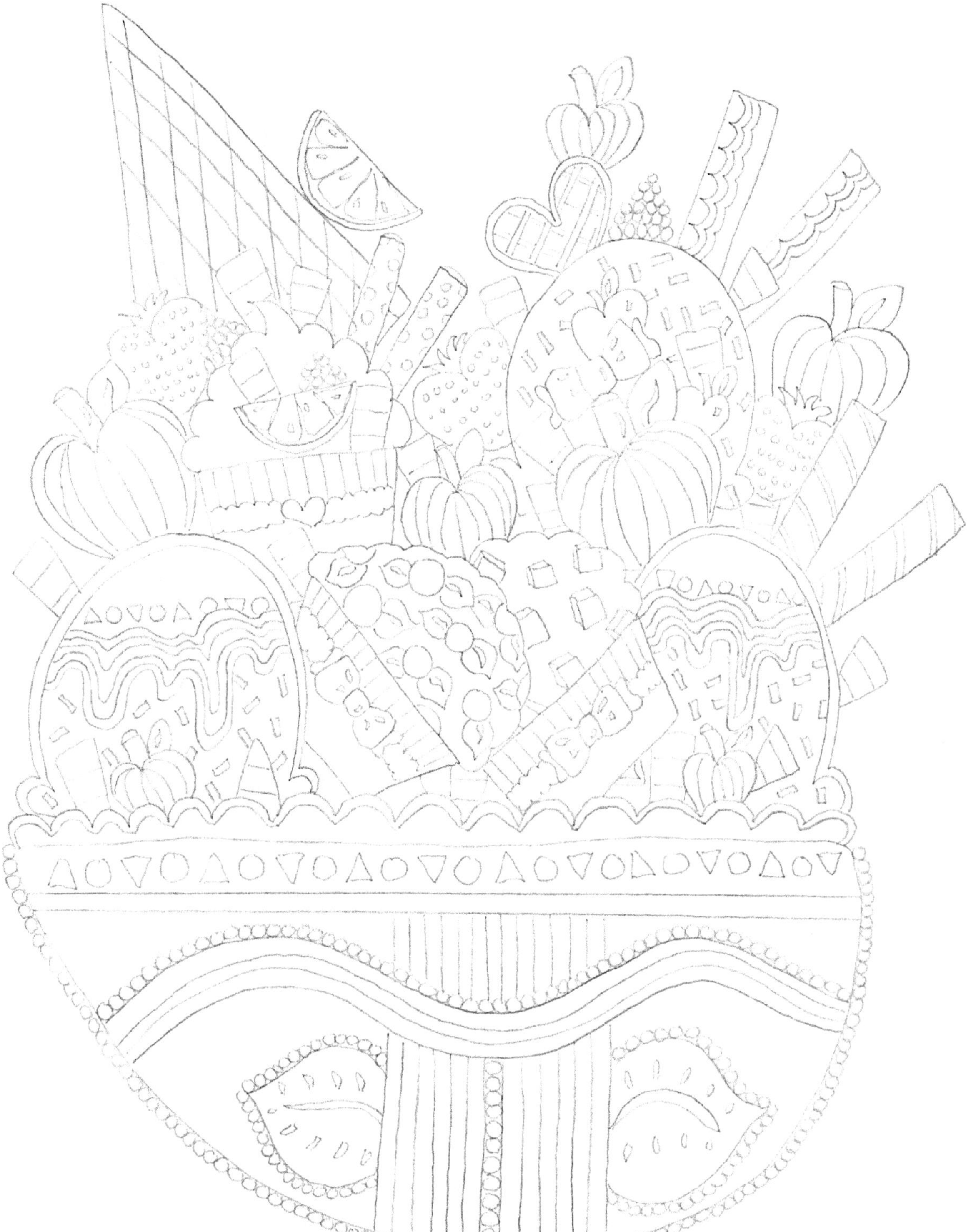

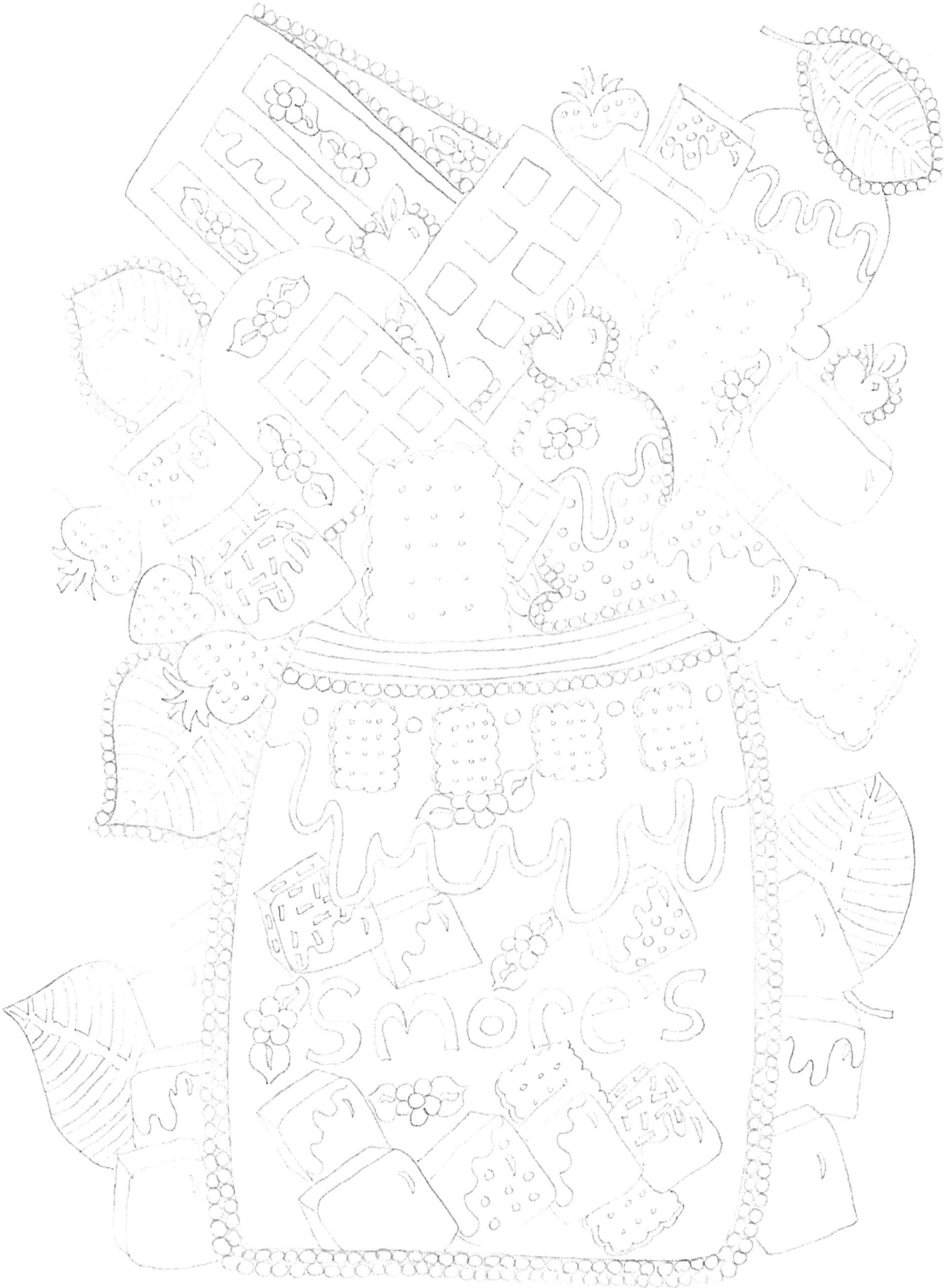
Smore's

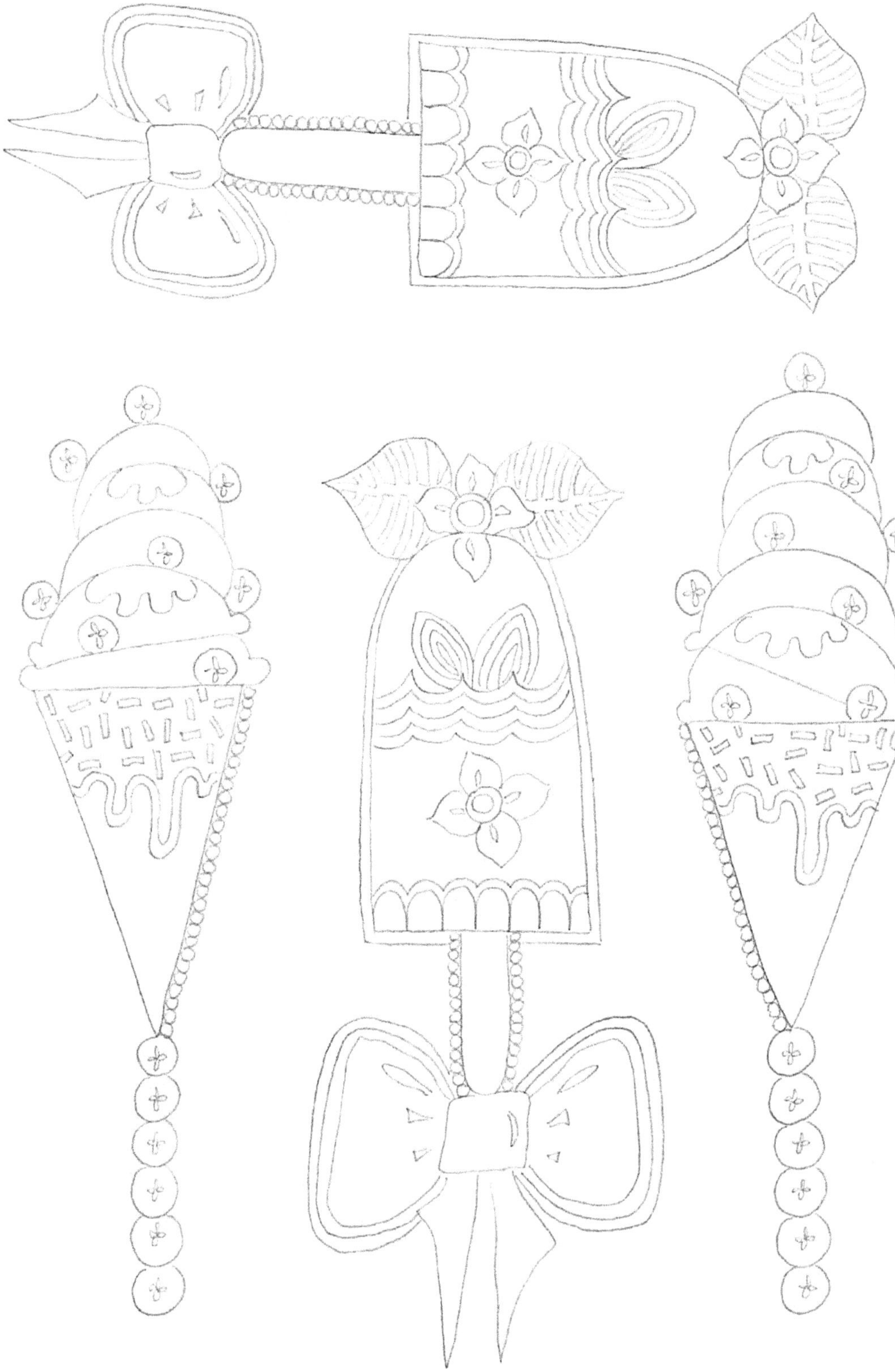

Italion
Cookies
Bowl

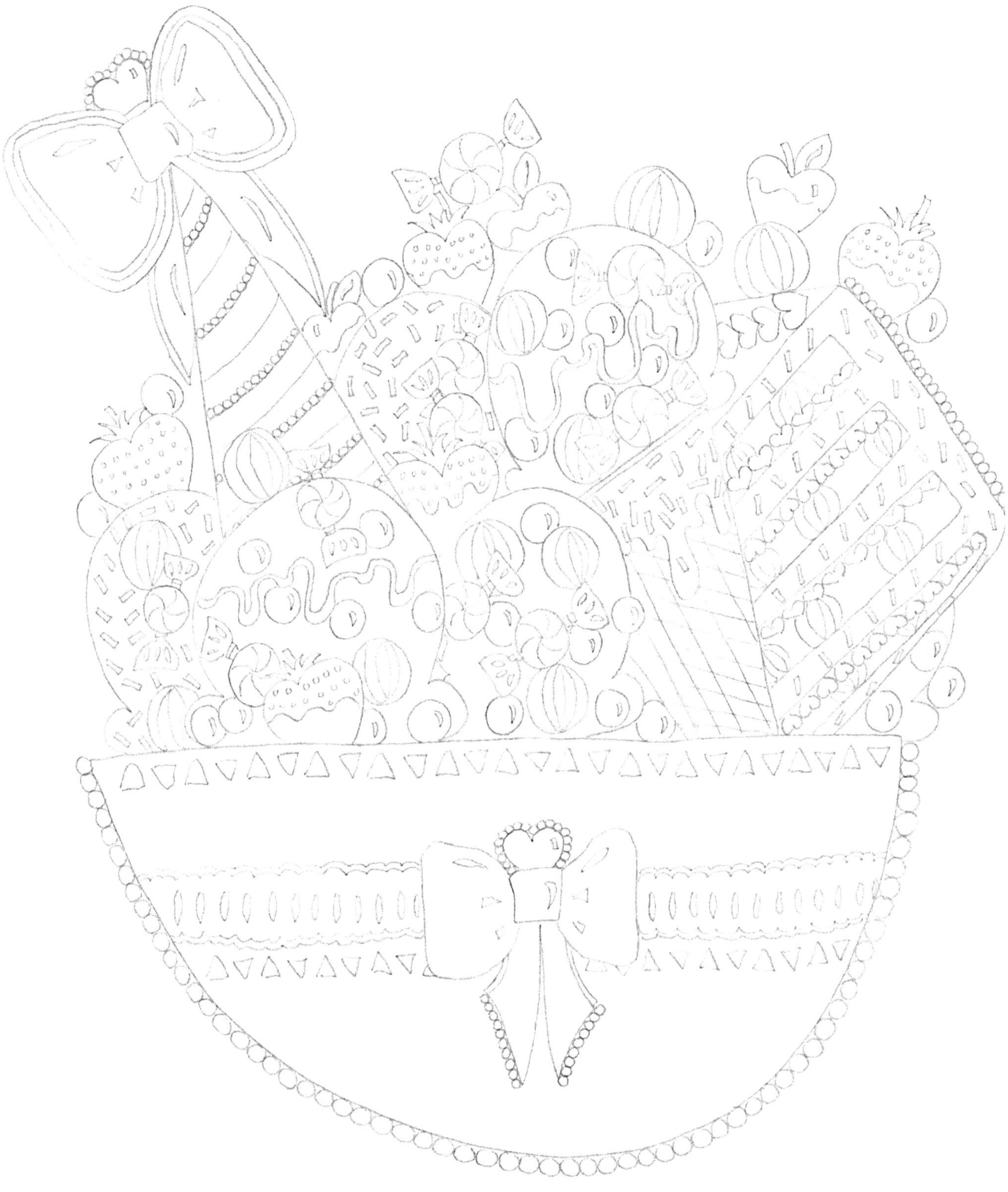

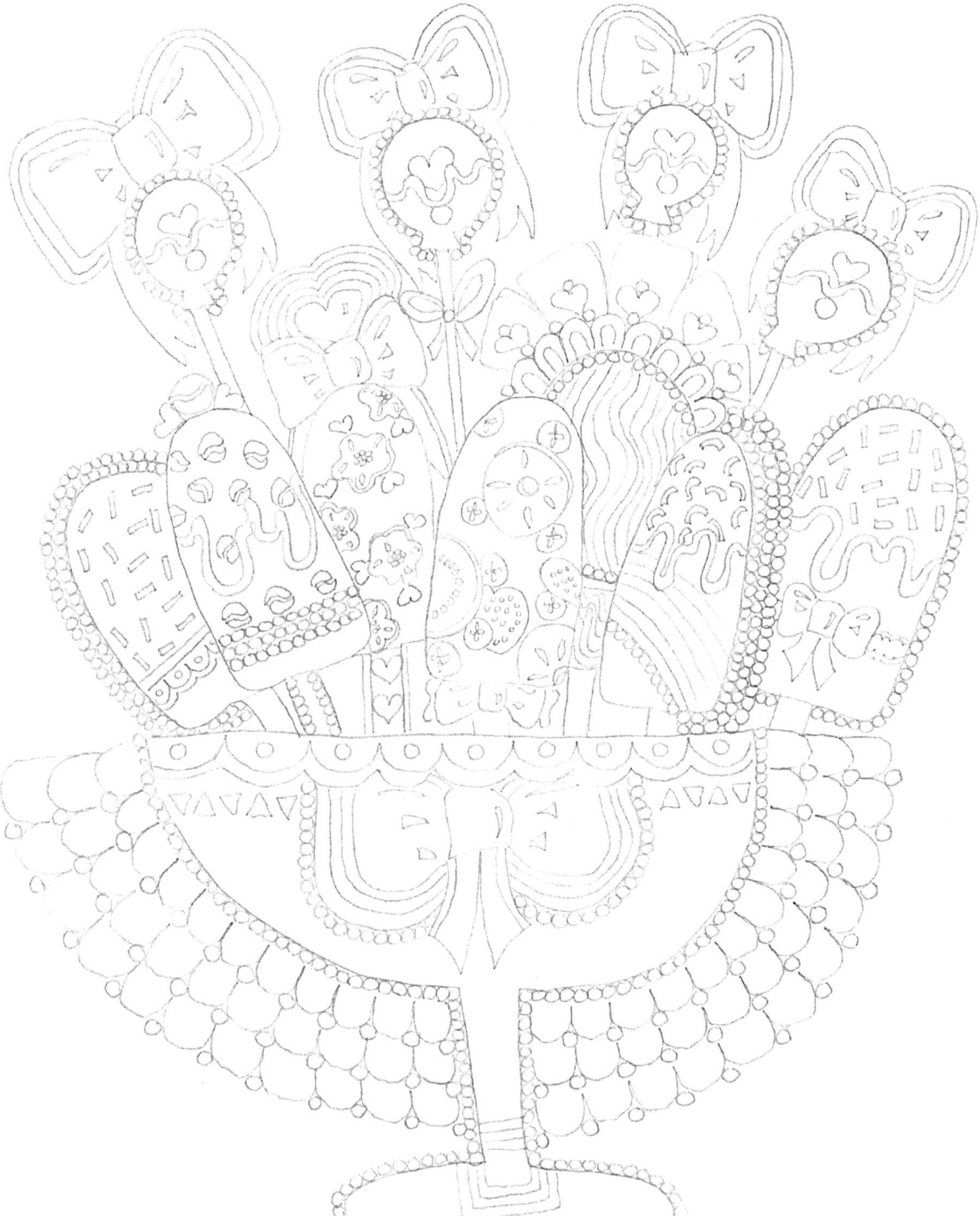

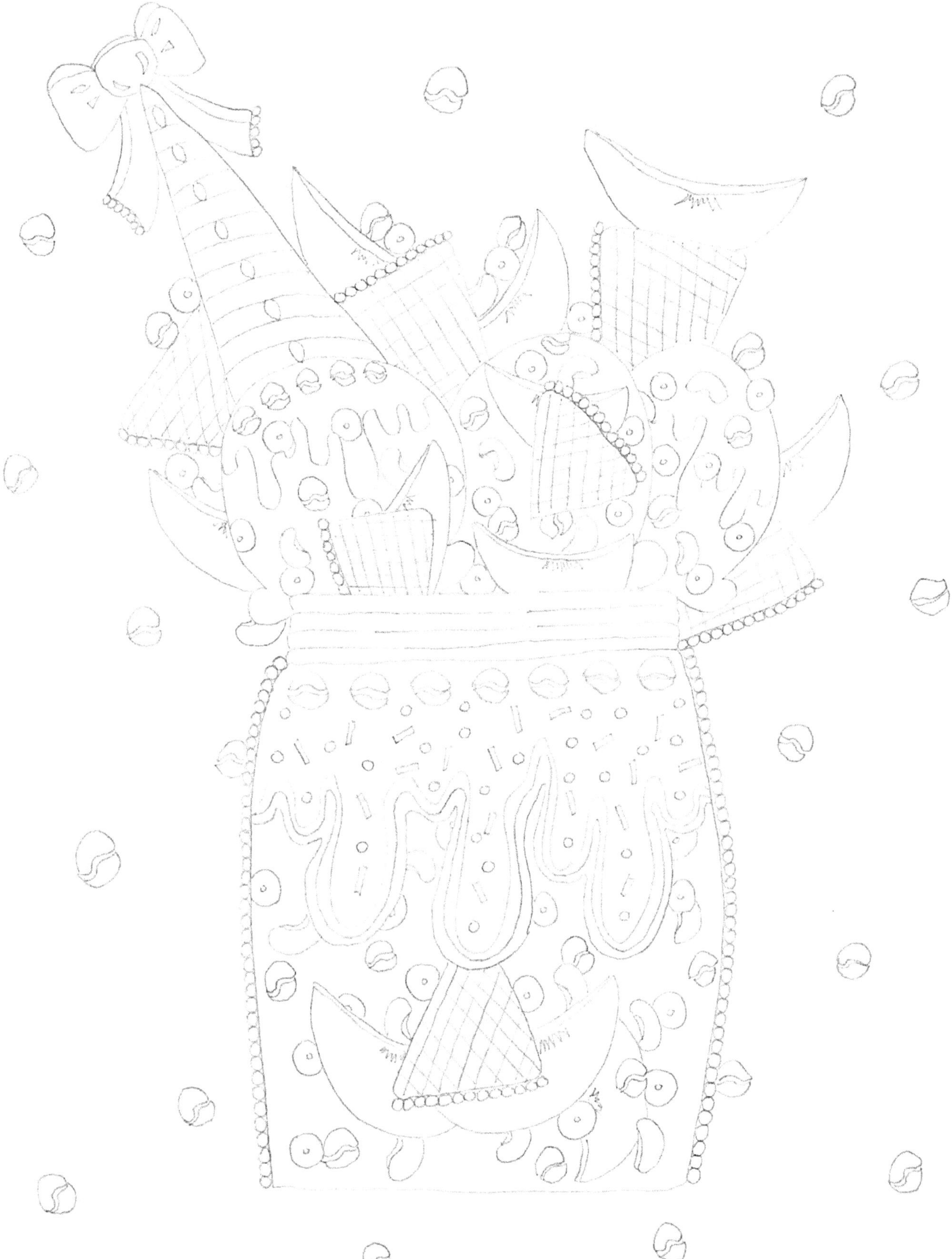

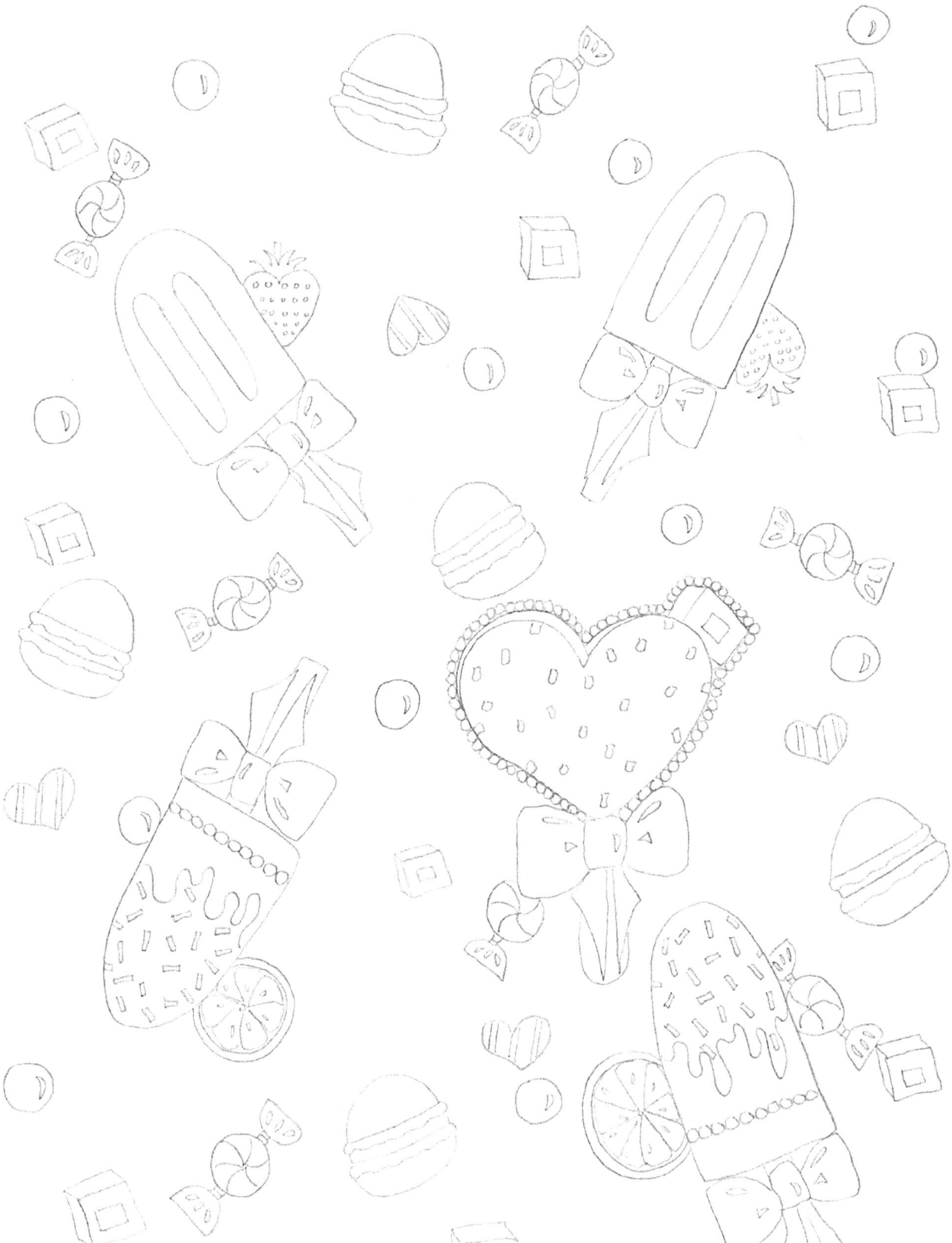

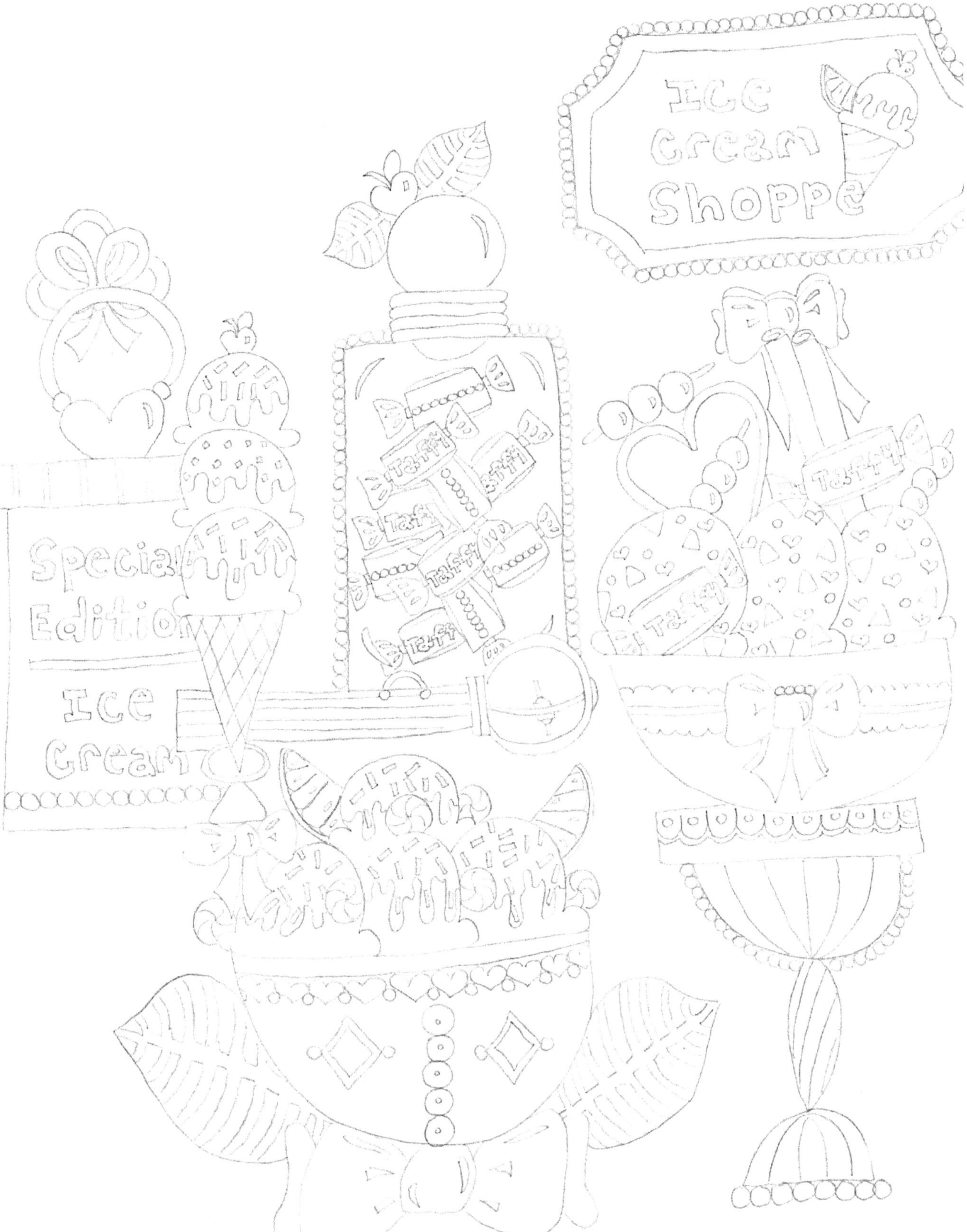

Ice Cream Shoppe
Special Edition
Ice Cream
Taffy

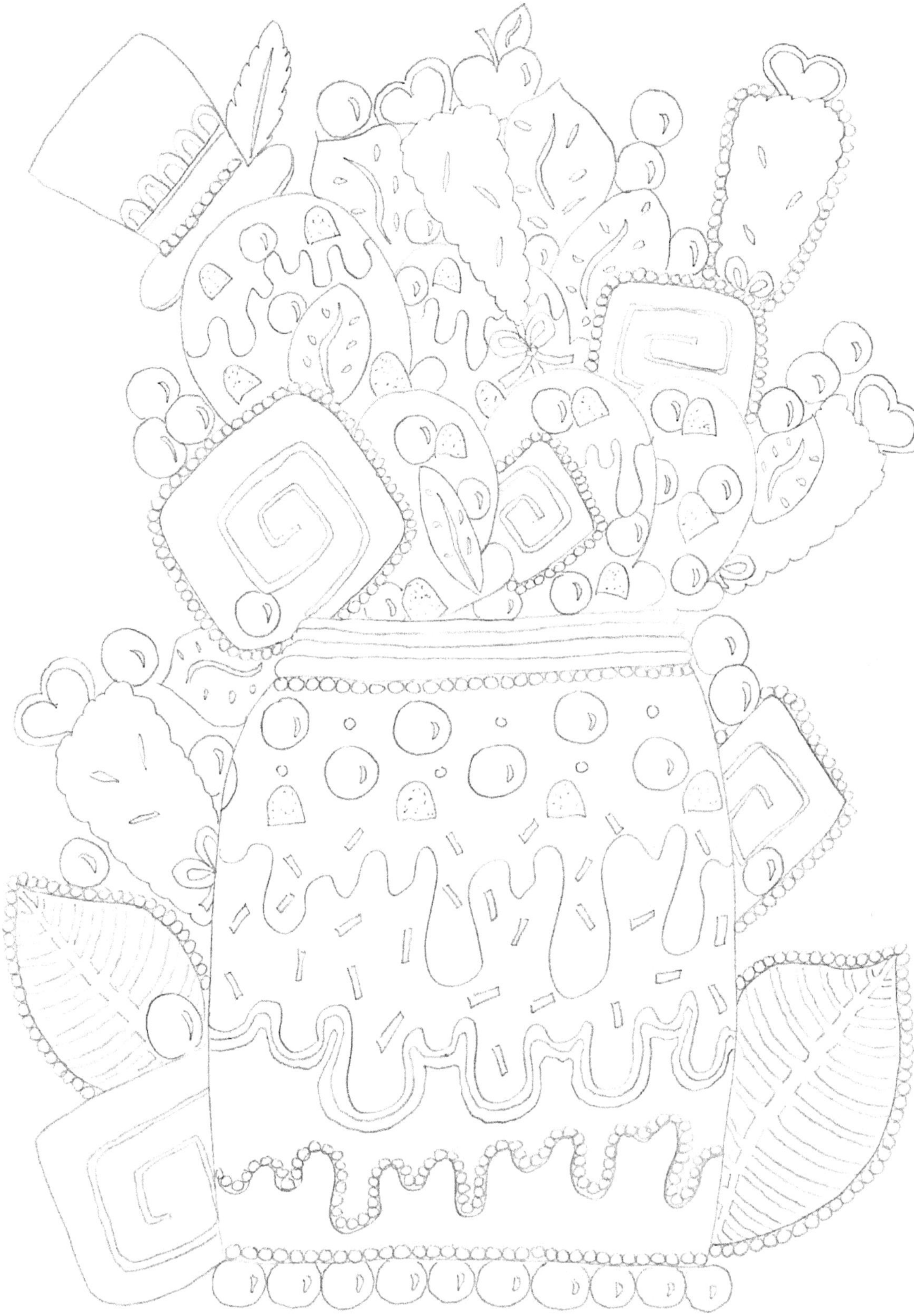

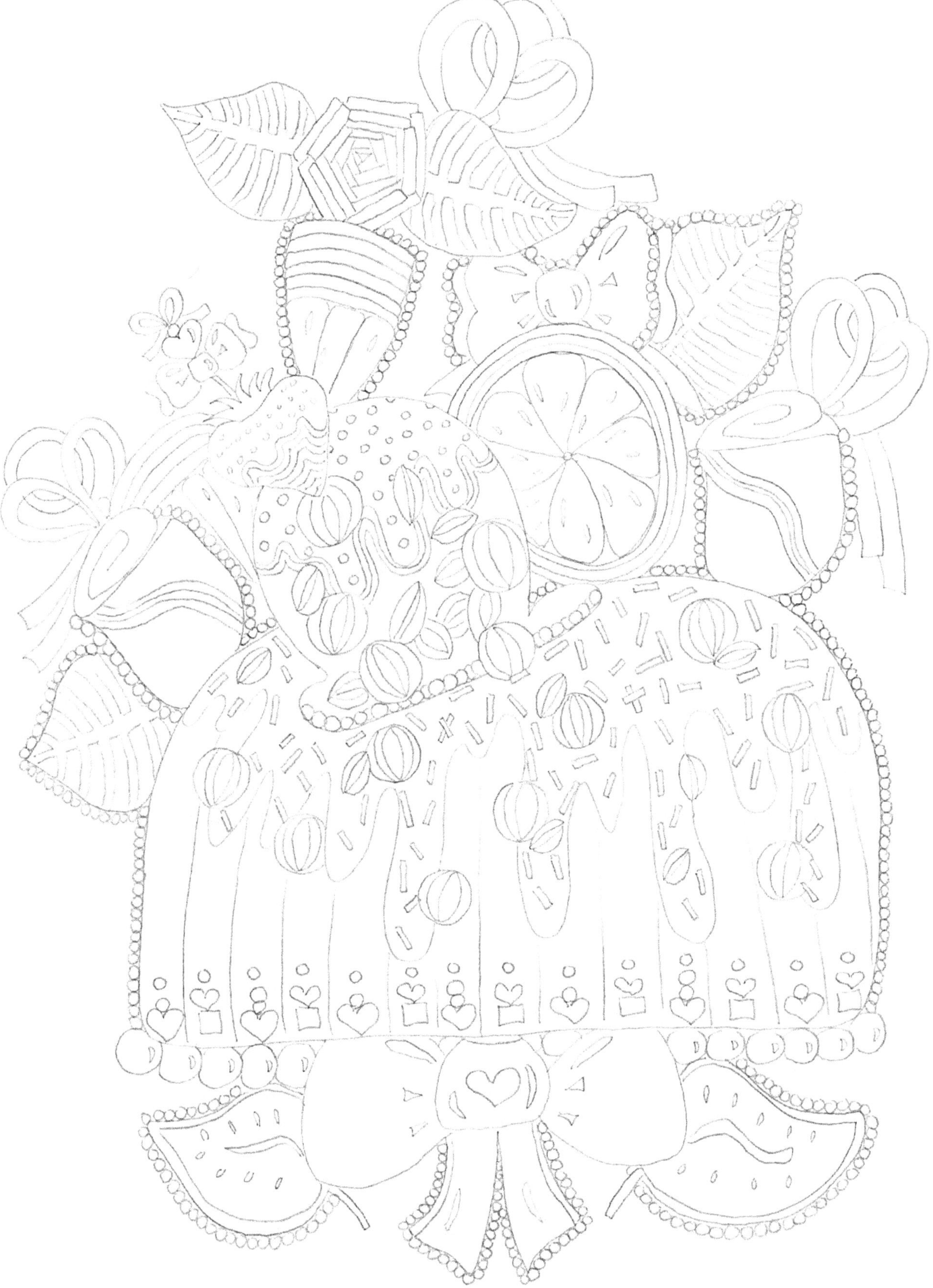

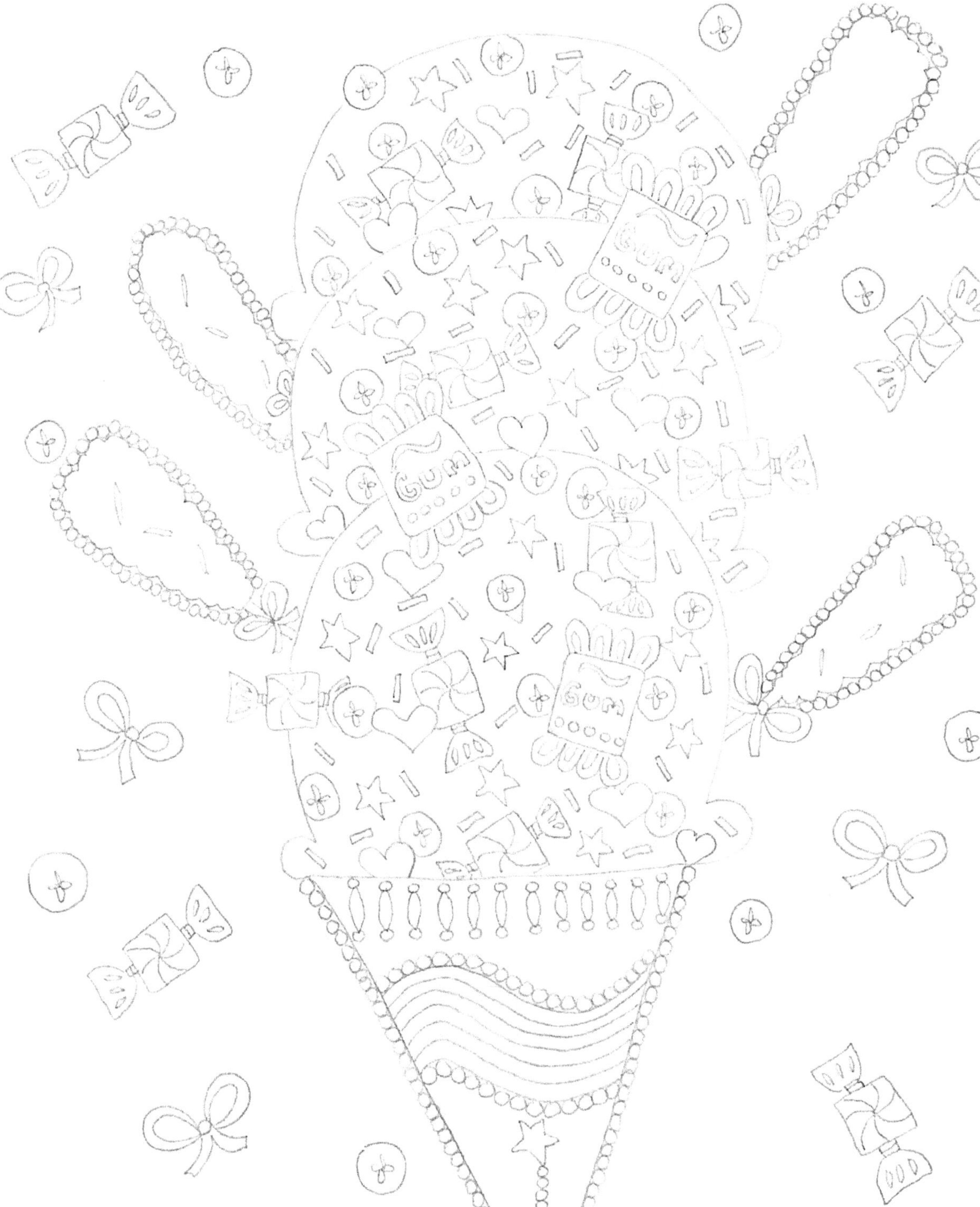
GUM
GUM
GUM

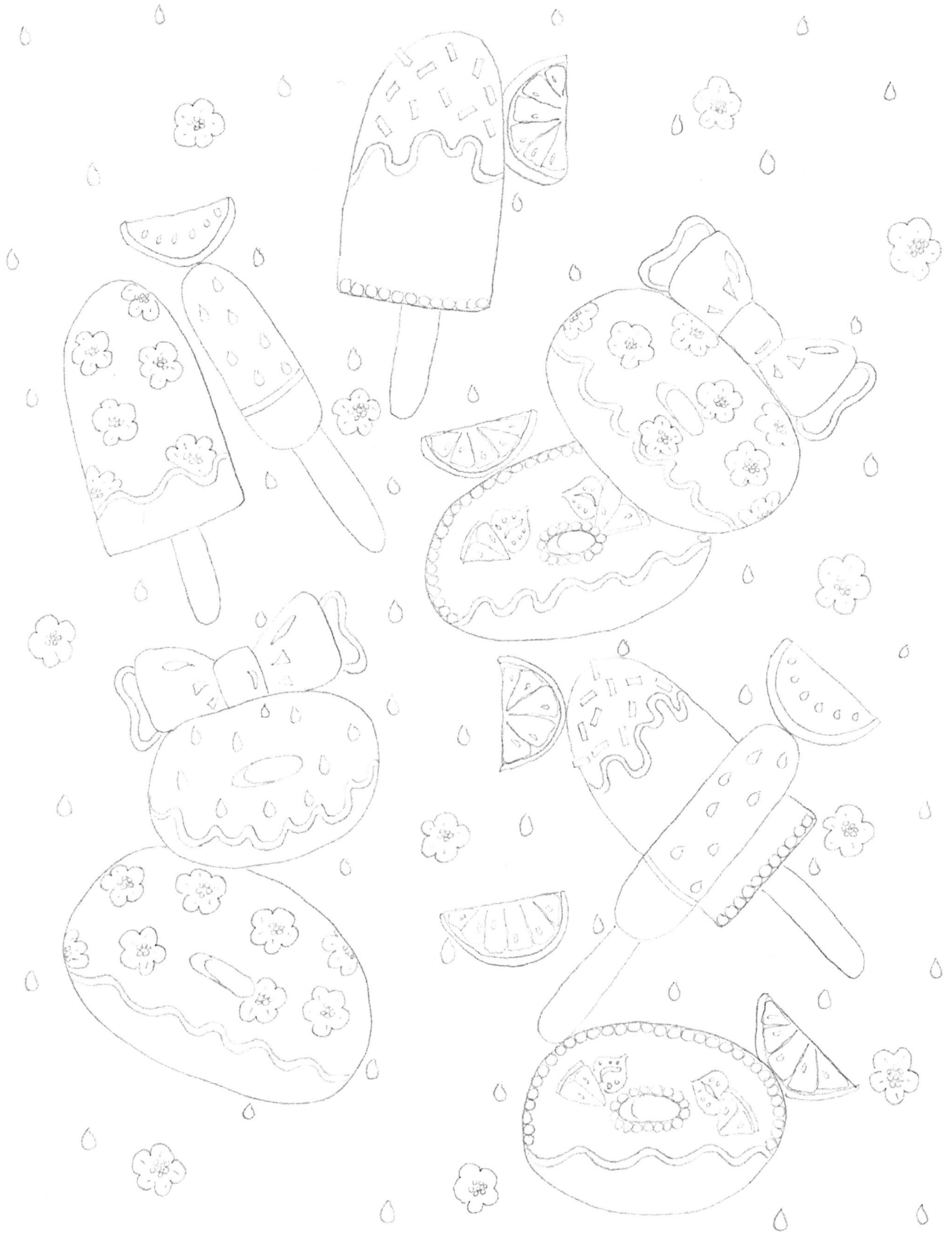

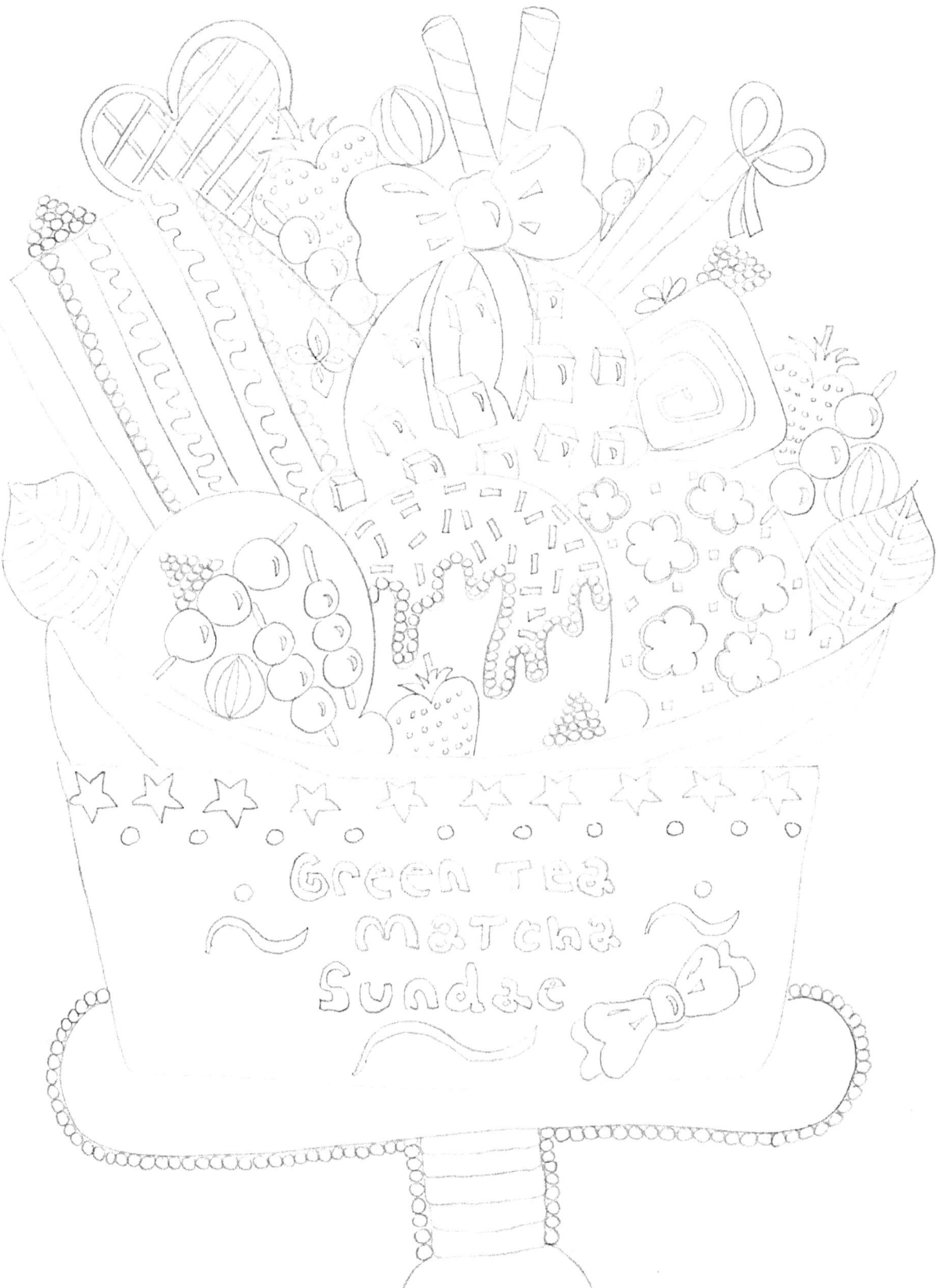
Green Tea
Matcha
Sundae

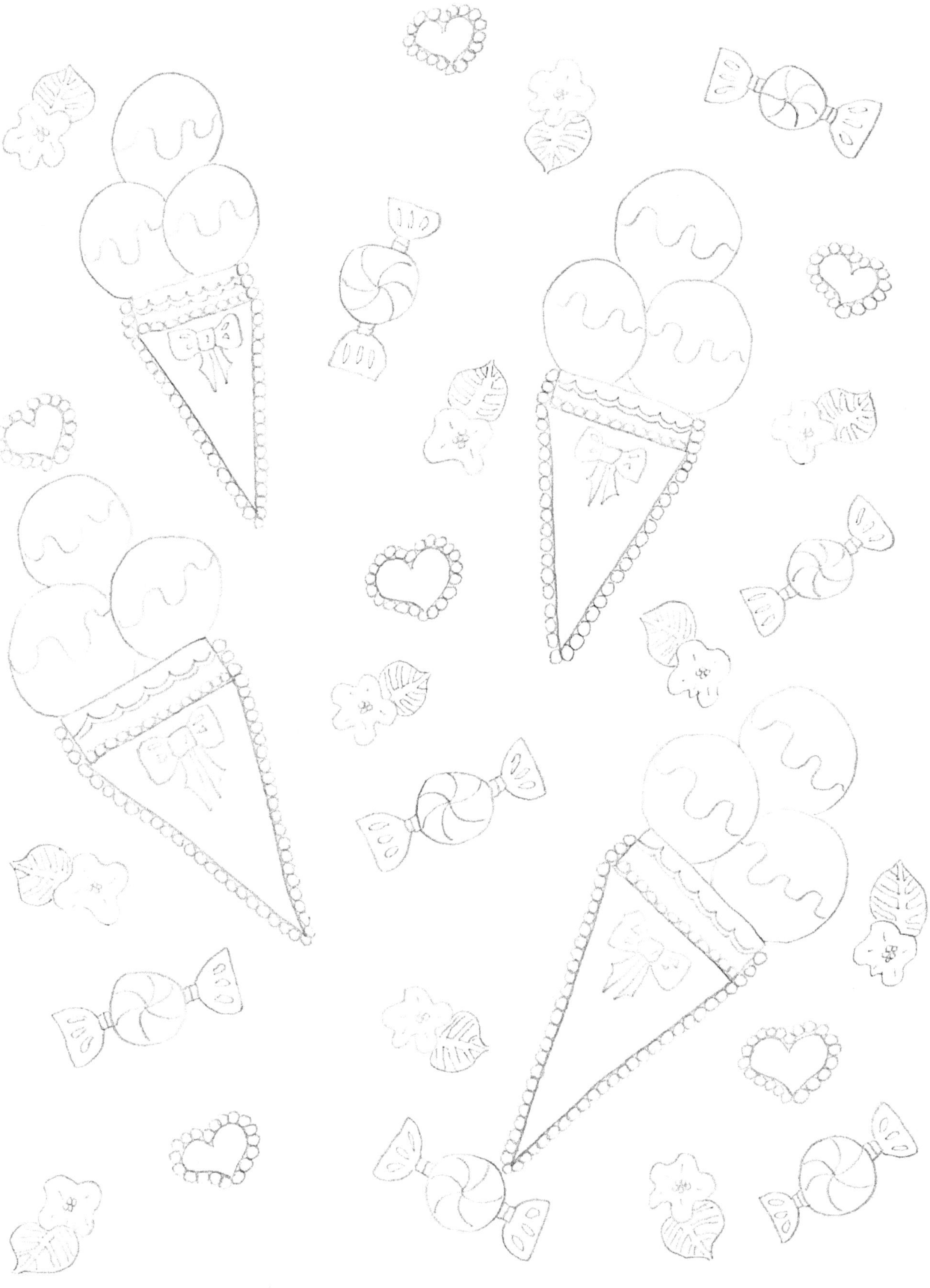

Chocolate
Sauce

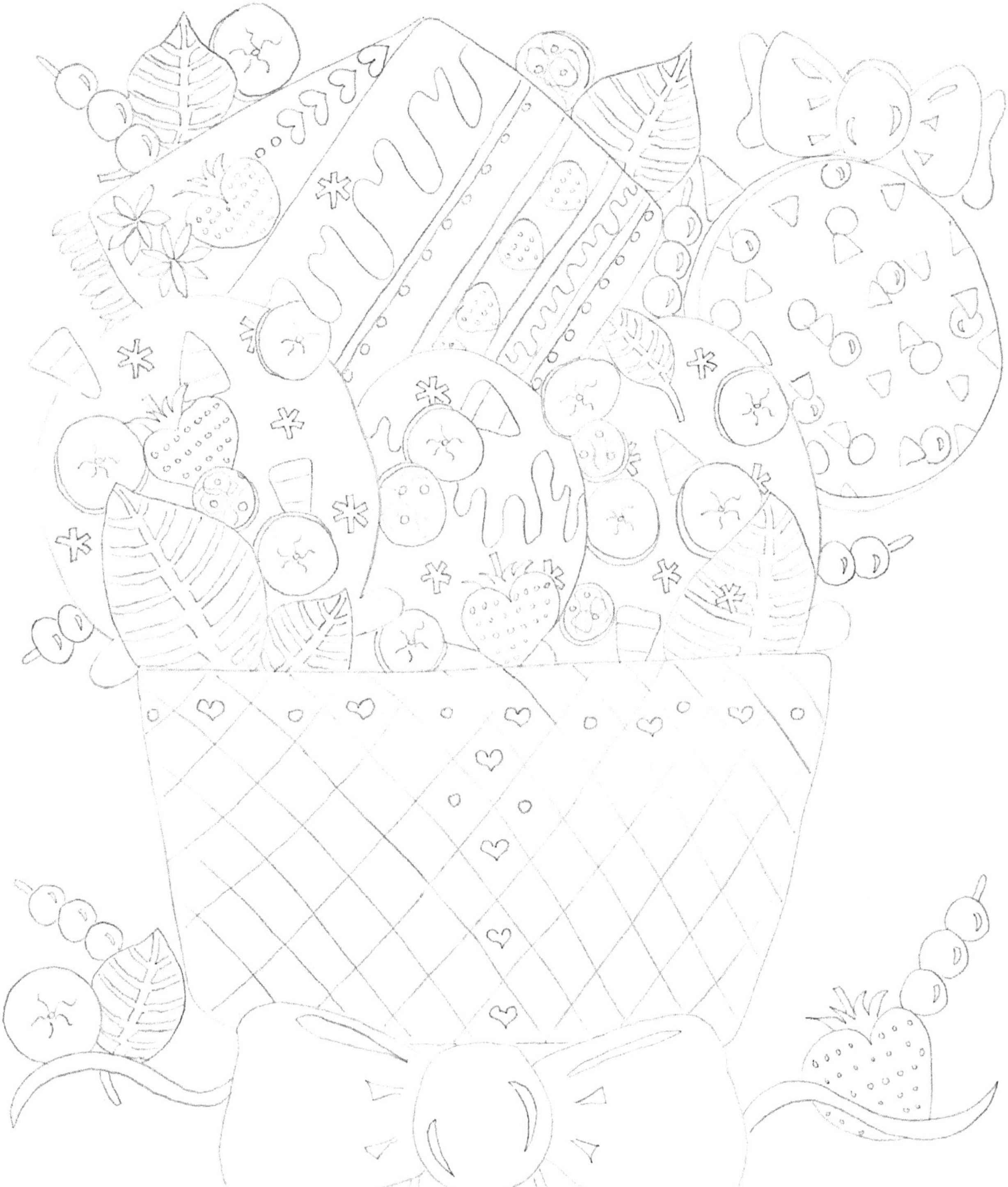

www.ingramcontent.com/pod-product-compliance
Lightning Source LLC
Chambersburg PA
CBHW060001230526
45472CB00008B/1902